THE UTTER ZOO AN ALPHABET BY EDWARD GOREY

🍎 Pomegranate

Portland, Oregon

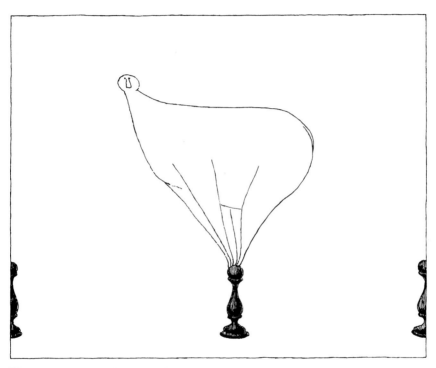

The Ampoo is intensely neat;
Its head is small, likewise its feet.

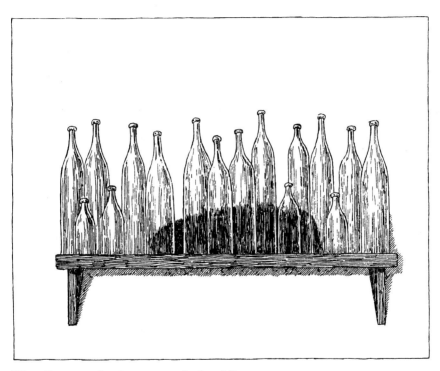

The Boggerslosh conceals itself
In back of bottles on a shelf.

The Crunk is not unseldom drastic
And must be hindered by elastic.

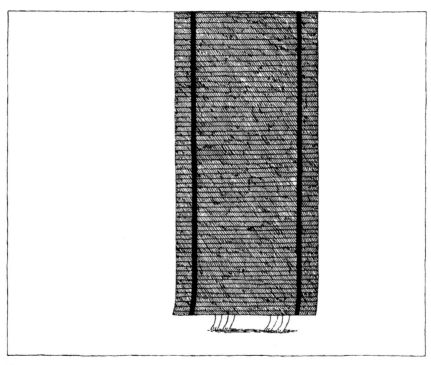

The Dawbis is remote and shy;
It shuns the gaze of passers-by.

The Epitwee's inclined to fits
Until at last it falls to bits.

The Fidknop is devoid of feeling;
It drifts about beneath the ceiling.

The Gawdge is understood to save
All sorts of objects in its cave.

The Humglum crawls along the ground,
And never makes the slightest sound.

The Ippagoggy has a taste
For every kind of glue and paste.

The Jelbislup cannot get far
Because it's kept inside a jar.

The Kwongdzu has enormous claws;
Its character is full of flaws.

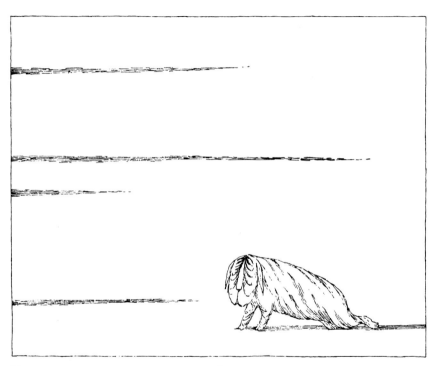

The Limpflig finds it hard to keep
From spending all its life asleep.

The Mork proceeds with pensive grace
And no expression on its face.

The Neapse's sufferings are chronic;
It lives exclusively on tonic.

The Ombledroom is vast and white,
And therefore visible by night.

The Posby goes into a trance
In which it does a little dance.

The Quingawaga squeaks and moans
While dining off of ankle bones.

The Raitch hangs downward from its tail
By knotting it around a nail.

The Scrug's extremely nasty-looking,
And is unusable for cooking.

The Twibbet on occasion knows
A difficulty with its toes.

The Ulp is very, very small;
It hardly can be seen at all.

The Veazy makes a creaking noise;
It has no dignity or poise.

The Wambulus has floppy ears
With which to wipe away its tears.

The Xyke stands up at close of day,
And then it slowly walks away.

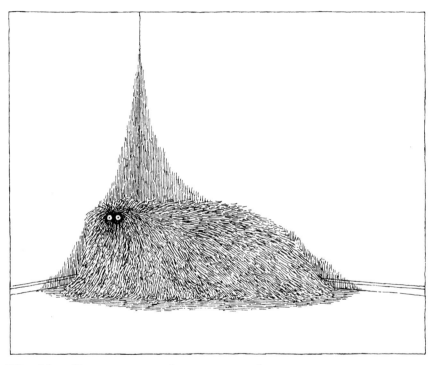

The Yawfle stares, and stares, and stares,
And stares, and stares, and stares, and stares.

About the Zote what can be said?
There was just one, and now it's dead.

Pomegranate Communications, Inc.
19018 NE Portal Way, Portland, OR 97230
800-227-1428   pomegranate.com

Pomegranate Europe
Number 3 Siskin Drive, Middlemarch Business Park
Coventry, CV3 4FJ, UK
+44 (0)24 7621 4461   sales@pomegranate.com

This edition first published by Pomegranate Communications, Inc., 2010.

Library of Congress Control Number: 2010921494
ISBN 978-0-7649-5508-2

Item No. A186

Designed by Gina Bostian

Printed in China
29 28 27 26 25 24 23 22 21 20   12 11 10 9 8 7 6 5 4 3

More Edward Gorey books from Pomegranate

The Adventures of Gremlin, by DuPre Jones
The Angel, the Automobilist, and Eighteen Others
The Awdrey-Gore Legacy
The Betrayed Confidence Revisited: Ten Series of Postcards
The Black Doll: A Silent Screenplay by Edward Gorey
Cobweb Castle, by Jan Wahl
The Donald Boxed Set
The Dong with a Luminous Nose, text by Edward Lear
The Eclectic Abecedarium
The Evil Garden
Edward Gorey: His Book Cover Art & Design, by Steven Heller
Edward Gorey: Three Classic Children's Stories
Edward Gorey: The New Poster Book
Elegant Enigmas: The Art of Edward Gorey
Elephant House: or, the Home of Edward Gorey, by Kevin McDermott
Floating Worlds: The Letters of Edward Gorey & Peter F. Neumeyer
The Hapless Child
The Lost Lions
The Osbick Bird
The Remembered Visit
Thoughtful Alphabets: The Just Dessert & The Deadly Blotter
The Treehorn Trilogy, by Florence Parry Heide
The Twelve Terrors of Christmas, text by John Updike
Why We Have Day and Night, by Peter F. Neumeyer
The Wuggly Ump

and don't miss . . .
    Edward Gorey's Dracula: A Toy Theatre
    Escape from the Evil Garden: An Edward Gorey Board Game
    The Fantod Pack
    The Helpless Doorknob: A Shuffled Story by Edward Gorey
    Mélange Funeste